THE DEVONSHIRE DIALECT

Being a collection of reminiscences, anecdotes, customs and traditions in which the Devonshire dialect is shown to be an important part of the character of the Devonshire people

BY
CLEMENT MARTEN

With occasional references to the counties of Dorset, Somerset and Cornwall

Included is a dictionary of over 800 dialect words and phrases with a guide to pronunciation and usage

Peninsula
Press

1973 Dedication

To my wife Olive with thanks for all her help

First published 1973 by Clement Marten Publications

Republished in 2002 by Peninsula Press,
an imprint of Forest Publishing
Woodstock
Liverton
Newton Abbot
Devon TQ12 6JJ

British Library Cataloguing in Publication Data

A catalogue record for this book is available from the British Library.

ISBN 1–872640–22–2

Printed and bound in Great Britain by:
Kingfisher Print & Design Ltd, Totnes, Devon TQ9 5XN

Introduction

My late husband's object in writing this book was twofold. Firstly to compile a dictionary of words and phrases used in the Devonshire dialect, with examples of their use, and secondly to show that the dialect was, and in some areas still is, a living and colourful part of people's lives. He felt that the best way to convey the latter was to write from a personal point of view from his own experience of the dialect and its use.

The words and phrases in the Dictionary conjured up his boyhood memories, reminding him of people, incidents or anecdotes. In retelling some of these, he tried also to give an insight into the minds of the Devonshire people - their attitudes and approach to the familiar and unfamiliar - their relations with each other and with the "vurriner". What is written is mostly the result of collecting words over the years and personal contact with the dialect and the people who spoke it - some still do! One of these, Sam Gilbert, was a waggoner on his uncle's farm at Whitstone, near Holsworthy. Another was an old sea captain, Cap'n Rickard, who lived at Oreston near Plymouth. But the one who above all educated him in the dialect was his Auntie Bea, who learned hers at Clawton Bridge, near Holsworthy, in the 1890s.

These, and many others, have all unknowingly contributed to this book and he was grateful to them for creating in him a love of the Devonshire dialect.

Olive M. Marten

The following account, written by Clem Marten for the Devon County Agricultural Association's Centenary Commemoration Book - 1872-1972, prompted him to research and write about the Devonshire dialect.

"A Prapper Day Out - Sure' nuff"

Yer! Did I ever tell 'ee 'bout the time us went to the vust Dem' County Shaw? Well 'twer a vew yer agon now, but I can mind it s'well as if twuz lass week. You zee zome o' the gentry - sech volk as Squire up to the big 'house an' zome gennelmen varmers got spaekin' 'bout 'avin' a get-together wer they cued shaw off zome of their 'osses an' cattle. Zeems they 'ad a bit of a maetin' an' wot wi' one an' t'other of 'em, they cummed up wi' the idaya of this yer Dem' County Shaw.

Well yew naws 'ow 'tis wi' the gentry, they 'as to do a maister lot o' talkin' vor they gets on wi' the job an' gets ort dood, but in the aend the gert day cummed. There wuz dree of us gwain - me missus, me cuzin Zpedigue wot varms over to Barnecott an' mezel. Me missus 'ad a bit of a bake-up een the cloam omm an' 'er dood zome tiddy an' mate pasties an' a vew tarts an' zich like an' rapped mun up een clane cloths an' packed mun een 'er market baskit ready ver the morning.

Us got got our milkin' dood a bit early - 'bout vive - an' off us goes wi' 'oss an' trap. Us cummed een over Cowley Bridge, pass the 'Pack 'Oss' an' up over North Street.

Now me missus zaid 'er did'n want ver to gaw traipsin' roun' the Shaw, lookin' at 'osses an' effers - 'er zeed they every day of the yer, 'er zaid. Wot 'er wanted du wuz leuk roun' the shaps wi' 'er zister wot lives een Exeter. Zo 'er got out corner 'igh Street an telled us to mate 'er een the zame place at zix o'clock. Down over Zouth Street us goes an' out to the Shaw Yard. 'Course, be this time there wuz a vew other volk wi' the zame idaya an' it tooked us a liddle wiles to get een, but when us did, us 'itched the 'oss an ztarted to 'av a leuk roun'.

My gar, you nivver zeed nort like it! Ver a ztart, there wuz the volks - I don't think I nivver zeed zo many volks all to one place een me live avore.

There wuz varmers like us all got up een their Zindy-go-to-Matin' britches an' leggins, there wuz the gentry wi' their top 'ats an cigars an' there wuz the drovers an zitch like een their zmocks wi' doags to 'eel. Us zeed a vew ladies roun', but most of they wen' off arter a bit to the shaps een Exeter - like me missus.

Well, like I zaid, us ztarted to 'av a leuk roun' but there wuz a maister lot to zee, us didn't 'ardly naw wot to leuk at vust. Anyways, us wuz near the pigs, zo us 'ad a leuk at the zows an' vears. Prapper viddy they wuz - all claned up an' washed ver the Shaw.

Then us wen on to zee the sheap. My gar, there wuz zome maister vine leuk-in' yaws an' rams een every breed. 'Course, us runs Longwools zo us wuz kane to 'av a gude leuk at they, but I mus' zay, the Dartmoors an' Exmoors an' Orns, as well as they Lesters, wuz all as purty as a picture. They wuz all zheared an' brished an' combed an' made suiant zo I don't naw 'ow the jidges could 'cide one vrum t'other or which wuz best.

'Bout this time, us cummed to a tent an' een thicky they wuz zelling zider an' beer, zo me an Zpedigue 'cides it wuz 'bout time us wets our oozles. Zo us 'ad one or two an' on agin to zee the cattle.

Az you'd 'zpect, they wuz mostly Dems, but there wuz a vew Zhortorns, an' zum of they Channel Ilans. Wot purty liddle bastes they wúz too - leuked too purty to be gude milkers, but they telled us that the milk be zo zwate an vull o' crame as yude nivver belave.

'Bout this time, they wuz jidgin' zum of the Zouth Dems een the ring, zo us 'ad a lane on the rail an' zeed they ver a bit.

Next, us thought us ud go an' 'av a leuk at the 'osses. Us ztarted wi' the ponies, but then us zeed the 'freshment tent zo Zpedigue an' me drapped een ver one or two ver to kape us gwain wile us wuz walkin' down drue the 'oss lines. There wuz zum bootivul gert stallions - Zuffolks, Clydesdales an' Zhires. There wuz mares an' voals, colts, geldins, 'acks an' a maister lot of ponies vrum all over Dem. Prapper brave show it made, an' the 'osses zeemed to naw there wuz zumthin' special gwain on the way they 'eld their 'aids up and ztepped 'igh.

Be this time, me an' Zpedigue wuz valein' us cud do wi' a bite t'ate, zo us goad over to the 'oss an' trap to get zum of me missus's pasties. Us put the veed bag on Dolly an' went to the 'freshment tent to 'av a vew wi' our dinner. Us zeed a lot o' volks us naw'd an' bein' a special day out, they buyed us a vew an' us buyed they a vew, an' wot wi' one an' t'other, us wuz valein' t'wuz 'bout time us walked it off a mite, zo off us goes to 'ave a leuk at the varm impliments, an' zo on.

Me an' Zpedigue wuz thinkin' of buyin' a vew new things, so us 'ad a gude leuk 'roun' at wot the different makers wuz offerin'. Zum o' the zellin' vellers 'ad a vew virkins of zider an' zum gin an' if they thought you wuz a zairious buyer, they gived ee a drap o' this or that, an' in the aend, us 'ardly naw'd 'ow to chooze. I wuz taken wi' wot Beares, down to Newton Abbot, 'ad got on shaw, zo I ordered a new Winnowin' Machine vrom they at eight poun' vive shillin'.

Een caze you zhould think that all the exhibitors cummed vrom Exeter an' roun', there wuz plenty vrom other parts o' Britain, an' even zeveral American virms. One o' they wuz the Zinger Manufact'ring Company. They wuz zellin' these yer machines ver to 'elp the wimmin volk an' maids to do the zewin', an' wuz priced vrum zix poun' ten zhillin' to thirty vive poun'! Gude job me missus wuzn't wi' us else 'er'd a wanted one o' they, but I thought I'd better get zumthin' ver 'er, zo I buyed 'er a new dree-legg'd cricket ver 'er to do 'er milkin', cuz one o' the legs of 'erz 'ad cummed out, an' erd valled een the dung an' zpilled half a bucket o' milk, zo I reckoned 'twuz a zort of' 'vestment as well as a present.

Be this time, us wuz valein' us 'ad 'ad nuff traipsin' roun', zo us went back to 'freshment tent where us zeed a vew more folks us naw'd. Well us buyed they a vew gins an' they buyed us a vew back. 'Course, it wouldn't nivver do to let me missus naw that I 'ad one or two when 'er wadden leukin' but then you got to let yerzel go now an' then, amn ee?

Now Zpedigue 'ad 'ad a drap or two more'n me zo I thought 'twer 'bout time I wuz gettin' ee 'omewards, zo I 'elped'n over to the 'oss an' trap. Afterwards, ee vowed an' declared ee wuz 'elpin me! Us went back dru Exeter an' 'long the Cowley Road an wot wi' the zound o' the 'oss's 'ooves an' the one or two draps o' this an' that, us 'ad 'ad us nodded off. 'Course, Dolly naw'd 'er way 'ome an' twuz only when 'er cummed een the yard an' stopped outside 'er ztable that us woked up. 'Twadden long vor us wuz t'bade an' zoun' a 'slape.

Me missus? Oh ace, I 'ad ver to go back to Exeter next day to 'er zister's, cuz I'd vergot all 'bout matein' 'er at six o'clock like 'er telled me. Didden I yer all 'bout it wen 'er zeed me! An didden I yer all 'bout it all the way 'ome! Oh ace you, I shan't nivver vergit the vust Dem County Shaw - me missus zees to that!

The Devonshire Dialect

D evonshire, like other counties, has its own rich dialect, much of it traceable to the Anglo Saxon tongue, but it would be wrong to suppose that there is one Devonshire dialect, or that pronunciations are uniform throughout Devon.

Furthermore, it would be equally wrong to think that the dialect comes to a halt when we cross the borders into Somerset, Dorset or Cornwall. The dialects of these counties merge with that of Devon near the borders and it requires an acute ear to decide when the pronunciations and intonations have become truly those of each particular county.

Just as words and idioms differ from one area of Devon to another, so the intonations differ. Intonation is as much part of the character of the Devonshire dialect as is pronunciation. To try to convey intonation, let alone differences, by the written word is beyond my ability and so I shall deal with the pronunciation of dialect in general terms, with occasional references to regional variations.

With the advent of "education" and the B.B.C., the speech of the Devonshire people of today is a somewhat "watered down" version of the dialect, although it must be said that one still finds examples of the old dialect in the more isolated districts. A visit to any cattle market on market day will reward the listener with some good broad vowels and an exchange of pleasantries and banter, which may be unintelligible to the "vurriner". I hope that after reading this book, he will be able to understand a little of what he hears.

Many of the words used in dialect are looked upon with amusement and are thought to be "quaint". Nevertheless, many dialect words are probably more pure and correct than the corruptions which make up our everyday modern speech. The study of the dialect of the Westcountry is more than an amusing pastime - somehow the dialect words seem to recall vague memories of time gone by and to form a point of very real contact with those people who populated our Westcountry, who lived, worked, quarrelled, suffered, built and left their mark around them. We see evidence of their having been here before us in the form of buildings, bridges and roads, but do we know them? Do we know how they lived their lives, what hardships they suffered, the trades they followed, the hopes they had?

In these days of Public Health Departments, Inspectors and Regulations and general consciousness of hygiene, how can we have any concept of the way, for instance, the sellers of food conducted their business? An example of this was to be found in Exeter's Butcher's Row, (now part of Smythen Street), where all the unsaleable offal, dung, etc., was heaped in the yards behind the shops. These rotting, stinking heaps were looked upon as valuable assets to be turned into cash when eventually sold as fertiliser. The owners of these offal heaps were highly indignant when they were forcibly removed as a measure to help contain the cholera epidemic, which not unexpectedly broke out in Exeter in 1832 resulting in something like 350 deaths. I mention this because it throws a light on the attitudes of the people, who only a few generations ago, live where we now live and used the dialect as their everyday speech. The dialect gives us some insight into these matters and one feels a little closer to them and their way of life, when one comes to examine the words and what lies behind them.

I would like to mention three people who have done much to keep alive the interest in the old speech of Devon. One of these, the author of a book of stories and poems, was Henry Baird, who listened to speech around him and set it down on paper. The book he wrote was entitled, *Letters and Poems tu es brither Jan, by Nathan Hogg*, (Baird's nom-de-plume). The book was dedicated to His Highness Prince Louis Lucien Bonapart, who apparently was greatly interested in the Devonshire dialect.

It is interesting to note that Henry Baird, who worked for a firm of wine merchants in Palace Gate, Exeter, must have been a town dweller with very little contact with country people. In the glossary of *Nathan Hogg*, there is scant mention of country words - he gives the Devonshire pronunciation of "elephant", but not of "horse". Even so, Nathan Hogg provides a wealth of information, not only with regard for dialect, but about people and the time - the soldiers and servants - the tradespeople and the "gentry". There is a copy of *Nathan Hogg* in the Exeter Reference Library and I have a copy on my desk. It was published by S.Draton & Sons.

Another author was William Weeks, who was a lecturer at the Exter Training College, (now St. Luke's School of Education, University of Exeter), where the students nicknamed him "Old Ball". He wrote a book entitled Bits o' Broad Devon, published by William Pollard in 1902. This book is now out of print, but there is a copy in the Exeter Reference Library and I also have a copy.

The other name I must mention is that of A.J.Coles, or "Jan Stewer", as he was known and loved by many thousands who heard him , or read his books. I remember as a child seeing him in Plymouth Guildhall, in the early days of "wireless" and the "cat's whiskers", where he gave a monologue in dialect on the subject to the great amusement of his audience.

Many years later, I was fortunate enough to meet Jan Stewer and "av a crack" with him in dialect in the Kings Arms, Tedburn St.Mary. He told me that he too, had a copy of *Nathan Hogg* on his desk and frequently referred to it.

Those who are interested in the Devonshire dialect should read "Jan Stewer" books, which contain so much that sheds light on the attitudes and thinking of the people, as well as a wealth of pronunciations, idioms and dialect words.

It has been mentioned that intonation is difficult to convey in the written word, but there is one aspect of the dialect, which, in a way, is allied to intonation and that is the stressing of words. This is an interesting factor of the dialect, which in a subtle way, throws light on the people of Devon and the Cornish, (or Cousin' Jackers), across the Tamar.

It is generally known that strangers, or visitors, to the two counties were, (and frequently still are), called "vurriners" - (foreigners). This word in times gone by did not necessarily mean someone from another country, but was just as likely to be applied to a person from another town or parish within the county, although in recent times, it has been reserved for those from without its borders. Now, the Devonshire, or Cornish native, being naturally suspicious of "vurriners", their ways, speech, clothes and in fact, anything with which the native was unfamiliar, when talking of "vurrin" matters, or when using an unfamiliar word, would signify disapproval, contempt or unacceptance of an idea, product or habit, by laying stress on the relevant word. Not only would he stress the word, but would probably also deliberately mispronounce it in a derogatory manner. This was done not so much in the hearing of the "vurriner", as in that his fellow Devonians, so that by this stress and mispronunciation, he let it be known that he did not " 'old wi' ", [hold with], the subject under discussion and that, more important still, was not trying to copy the "vurriner".

Apart from the deliberate mispronunciation, there are those words which have been created through misunderstanding, or from the invention of words, which are imitations of words used by the "gentry" or clergy. These factors have contributed to a dialect of great richness, variety and sometimes, unconscious humour.

I can remember an old gentleman, in early days of wireless, complaining about the aerials which were being erected. Aerials in those days were pieces of wire strung between a tall pole in the garden and the house, then leading down by means of insulators into the house. The old gentleman disliked the idea of wireless in general and the forest of aerial poles sprouting over the land in particular. He said, "I can't abide aul thaise yer aul *hairy oils*."

Here is an example of a Devonshire man expressing his dislike by deliberately mispronouncing and stressing the words. This is a very subtle deliberate mispronunciation, because the use of "hair oil" would be frowned upon as a habit only indulged in by "vurriners" and the "gentry". The words "hairy oil" therefore, have a sort of double connotation, simultaneously expressing dislike of aerials and hair oil! Some of the younger "sparks" might, however, use a bit of lard on festive occasions.

A fertile source of examples of the dialect was the "Laukel Praicher" [Local Preacher], who preached at various chapels in a 10-15 mile radius of his own village, but I must pause here to explain that much of Devon and most of Cornwall was, and to an extent still is, "Chapel" [Wesleyan or Methodist], and the further West one goes the more numerous become the little village chapels, some of them apparently out in the wilds, but forming a focal and gathering point for the "chapel" people of the district.

The "laukel praicher", "Methody praicher" or "Rounder", was looked upon as something of a social catch when he came to one's village because it was customary for him to be the guest of one or two of the local households. The children of the chosen house would be in a fever of excitement and the housewife would be busy on Saturday preparing for the guest. Nothing would be done on Sunday which could be avoided - any activity, other than those which were essential, like milking, was "ungodly" and frowned upon. If my grandmother, who was "chapel" forgot to cut the cabbage from the garden on Saturday, we went without it on Sunday. And so the preparations were all but complete on Sunday morning in readiness for "praicher".

Sometimes he had his midday dinner in one house and his tea in another, but possibly, if his hospitality was provided at the house of a prosperous farmer, he would have both meals there. Naturally on these occasions, the best china came out, the lace tablecloth was used and extra large bowls of clotted cream were in evidence, to say nothing of three kinds of cake at tea time - "seedy", "saffron" and "dough". Occasionally he brought his wife and even one, or two children, all of whom were carefully scrutinised and commented on by the congregation in Chapel.

Some of the "laukel praichers" were looked upon as star attractions and when it was known that Mr ... was to "praich", you could be quite sure of a "full house", especially for the Evening Service. Fire and brimstone were preached and the gimlet eye seemed to look straight at one and even right through! When he referred to "the sinner in our midst", we children knew to whom he was referring, it was one's self! The mystery was, how *had* he found out?

One of these "praichers" habitually spoke in broad Devon and was preaching on the subject of the difficulty that would be experienced by a rich man attempting to get to heaven, giving the example of the camel going through the eye of a needle. He stopped in mid speech, realizing that camels passing through eyes of needles was not in the usual everyday experience of the congregation.

He said, "Yer, tidden naw gude ver me to be tellin' ee bout *camels* gwain drew hies o' *naedles* - yu wudden naw nort bout they. I'll putt it tu ee lak this yer, zo's yu can unnerstan'. Tiz aizier ver an aul cow to climmie up a tray an' cavvie een a craw's nest, than tiz ver a urch man t'ainter 'Eb'm." [It is easier for an old cow to climb a tree and give birth to a calf in a crow's nest, than it is for a rich man to enter Heaven.] The congregation understood and the story has passed into the folklore of North Devon.

On another occasion, the locality had been suffering from a prolonged drought - the crops were failing and it was difficult to water the cattle. The local preacher who was visiting the village on the Sunday was asked to pray for rain. He did so at the morning service and again during the afternoon service and still the sky was cloudless.

At the evening service he put all the eloquence he had into his plea for rain, pointing out to the Almighty that the crops were spoiling, the cattle were thirsty, the milk yield down and that the welfare of the community was at stake - (he was also a farmer). As he prayed, a wind sprang up and the more he prayed the stronger became the wind. Soon the rain came - it came down in sheets and the wind blew even stronger, so strong in fact, that the Chapel doors were blown open allowing the rain to drive in with great force. The preacher, who had been carried away with the quality of his own eloquence, suddenly stopped when the doors burst open. He looked up to Heaven and said, in a rather pained voice, "Oh Louard, 'ats *raydiclus!*" [Oh Lord, that's ridiculous!]

Gregory Harris in *Sketches of the West Countree*, 1905 quotes:"'I ventured to ask how the preacher had got on. 'Fust rate', replied the delighted hearer 'Proper sarmun an'no mistake.' 'What was it all about?' I asked. My friend scratched his head and at last replied, 'Well now, I be dalled if I kin tell ee zackly what twuz about, altho' twuz a rate trate, an no mistake; the words poured out ov un like watter out of a bukkit, but there!' he added by way of excuse for his want of definiteness as to the subject matter of the discourse - 'but there, twer ter'ble 'ot, and us was vive in a sait, so I s'pose twadden possible to car' away much when y'um crammed up like that there'.'"

" **T**he Exmoor Scolding and Courtship", believed to have been written by the Rev. William Hole, B.D., Archdeacon of Barnstaple in 1744 and first published in *The Gentleman's Magazine* in 1746, depicts very vividly the way of life in those days through written dialect. Apparently there were a number of editions of "The Scolding", one of which was edited by F.T.Elworthy, in 1876, in which he maintains that modern English has descended from the speech of the Midlands [of England], because of the great influence of three notable men on the English language through the written word. They were Wycliffe, Chaucer and Caxton, Midlanders who wrote, or printed, in the tongue of their time, using pronunciations, and therefore, spellings, familiar to them, which eventually evolved into our modern standard English.

Elworthy was of the opinion that had these men come from Southern England, it would have been correct, [in 1876], to say:
"The vield was zowed with zeed - you can zee how vast it do growey". No doubt we, a hundred years later, would probably be speaking in a similar manner.

There is written evidence that words which are now looked upon as being dialect, are traceable to very early times, but some are nevertheless, still in use by country folk today.

Here is a short list of some of these words, with their original spelling and the dates when they were known to have been in use.

1220	vor	..	for	1387	vair	..	fair
	vlize	..	flies		veaw	..	few
	vifte	..	fifth		vyzte	..	fight
1300	verst	..	first		dude	..	did
	vaste	..	fast				

A number of dialect words commonly used early in this century, some of which are still in use, are traceable at least to about 1750 and were, without doubt, used long before.

Rules

The Devonshire dialect has some rules which, although subject to variation, do occur fairly consistently. Additionally, there are several idiosyncracies which are so consistently followed, as to become rules in themselves. Firstly there is the use of the tenses. Almost invariably the past tense is accomplished by the simple expedient of tacking on "d" or "ed" to the end of a verb, as in the following examples:

"The lill tacker rinned vore th' raud" - [The little boy runned (ran) along the road.]

"Ers a gude lill maid - 'er'v aited up aul 'er dinner" - [She is a good little girl - she has eated (eaten) up all her dinner.]

"Er'v gaw'd awm" - [She has go'd (gone) home.]

The present tense never includes the word "are", but instead uses "is", "be" or "am", as in these examples:

"Us is gwain awm" - [We are going home.]

"Us be gwain awm" - [We are going home.]

"They'm gwain awm" - [They am (are) going home.]

The future tense is accomplished with "will" or "shall" in the form of "ll", as for example:

"Us'll be gwain awm" - [We will, or shall, be going home.]

Another idiosyncracy is to use " 'er " [her] when speaking of female *or* male and is frequently applied to inanimate objects. Here are some examples:

Female: "Av'er vinished 'er mulkin eet?" [Has she finished her milking yet?]

Male: "Av'er vinished ees mulkin eet?" [Has he finished his milking yet?] This could also be expressed: "Av'm vinished ees mulkin eet?" [Have him finished his milking yet?] Either form could be used, even in the same district.

Object: "Thick aul cricket baent naw gude - 'ers scat". [That old milking stool is no good she (it) is broken.]

A Devonshire saying is:

"In Dem, ees a er an' ers a ee, all 'cept th' aud Tom cat an' even ees a er!" [In Devon, he is a her and she is a he, all except the old Tom cat and even he is a her!]

I hope that clarifies the matter!

Pronunciations

T he use of a recognised form of phonetic spelling has been avoided, as this tends to be difficult to follow and is somewhat academic - which this book does not pretend to be.

However, a simple form of phonetic spelling has been evolved, which should assist the reader when examining the Dialect Dictionary.

"a" is pronounced as in "ham".

"aa" a long sound with a slight nasal quality like a sheep bleating, but without the quivver in the voice. There does not seem to be an equivalent sound elsewhere in the British Isles, but it does have echoes of the nasal sound in the French language.

"ai" is pronounced as in "pain".

"d" is frequently used in place of "th" - "datch" [thatch], "drashin' " [thrashing], "drexil" [threshold].

"e" as the first letter of a word is sometimes pronounced as "i" - "ivery" [every].

"e" as the first letter of a word is also pronounced "ae" - "aend" [end].

"e" in the middle of a word is always pronounced as "ai" [as in pain] - "rail" [real]. Some dialect speakers would make this and similar words sound "ray-ole".

"f" is usually pronounced as "v" - "vust" [first], "vew" [few].

"h" When an aspirate [h] preceeds a vowel at the commencement of a word, it is invariably dropped, which is common in other parts of Britain. Quite often the "h" is tacked onto the beginning of a word to give it emphasis, as in the following example of a woman shouting to her husband who had lit a bonfire in the garden, causing dense and smelly smoke - "Yu gurt vule, wad'ee wanna lit thicky aul vire ver? Yu'm maakin' a prapper dirty aul smitch aul *hovver* me clane claws wat I've jist 'anged out" [You great fool, what did you want to light that fire for? You are making a proper dirty old smoke all *over* my clean clothes which I've just hung out.] The word "hovver" would be stressed and even greater force given to it by the addition of the "h".

Sometimes the "h" is added to a word according to the whim of the speaker, who knows that there should be an occasional "h" dropped in somewhere in "polite" speech. A shining example of this was an old lady I knew named Miss Thompson. She would greet me with: "M'hornin

Z'hur, nice m'hornin this m'hornin Z'hur." She was known affectionately and privately to my family as: "Miss T*h*ompson".

"i"   is often used in place of "u" or "oi" - "jidge" [judge], "jine" [join]. It is also pronounced as "a", so that the word "file" could be "vile" or "vale". Both these words and others like them, could be pronounced "vi-ole" or "va-ole".

"m"   is often substituted for "n" at the end of a word. Devon becomes "Dev'm", "Deb'm" or "Dem". Heaven - "Hem". The substitution also occurs in the middle of some words:- evening could be either "aivnin" or "aivmin".

"o"   is sometimes "a" as in "Garge" [George].

"oo" is pronounced as in the Scottish "guid" [good].

"r"   It is another idiosyncracy of the South-West dialect, that where the letter "r" occurs it frequently changes places with the letter which follows it. For instance, "run" becomes "urn", "red" becomes "erd", Richard becomes "Urcherd" or "Urchet", "bridge" becomes "burge" and so on. This reversal is common in the dialect of Cornwall, Devon, Somerset and Dorset. Words in the dictionary with this "r" reversal are indicated "r".

"s"   as the first letter, and often in the middle of a word, is pronounced "z".

"s"   when coupled with "h" or "k" is occasionally pronounced as "x" - "ax" [ash or ask]. *See* "axwaddler".

"t"   is sometimes used in place of "d" as in the following example: "I gid'n a lent o' me 'oss" [I gived him a lend of my horse].

"th" as the first two letters, would be pronounced as in "thine" or as "d" - "thicky" [this] or "datchin" [thatching]. Never pronounced as in "think". Quite often "th" at the beginning of a word is dropped altogether, - "mower'n'at" [more than that]. This also applies to "th" at the end of a word, - "wi' iss yer datchin reed" [with this here thatching reed]. Incidentally, "wi' " is pronounced "wee". Like other parts of Britain - especially the London area - "th" in the middle or end of a word, if sounded, is done so as "v" or "f", - "vevvers" [feathers], "Plymuff" [Plymouth].

"u"   is occasionally pronounced as "i" or "ou" - "jist" [just], "joug" [jug].

Dialect Dictionary

ABBREVIATIONS: m   mispronunciation
                   rr   "r" reversal
                   (date) words traceable to the date indicated but which
                            were undoubtedly in earlier use. Other words not
                            indicated may be just as old but have not been dated

abroad broken, in pieces, burst open - "scat'n abroad" [broke it into pieces].

ace, ees, iss yes

addled rotten, "addle aided" [slow witted] "addled" eggs - stale or bad eggs

aend, aen end

age-traws hedge troughs, ie. ditches running beside hedges for drainage

agin against

aich each

aid head. A sheep drover would call to his dog - "git aid", meaning "get ahead" or "go in front" of the flock to stop or turn the sheep.

aikle equal

ails eels

aither either

aive heave - to throw, lift, push, pull

aivmin evening

aizy easy

aizy cheer easy chair

all haul

amezez hames - part of the harness of a working horse

amn'ee haven't you

angshus anxious

ankcher handkerchief

Anniversiry claws clothes to be worn on "Anniversary Day" - the day of the founding of the local Chapel or Sunday School. *See* **Zindy-go-to-Matin**

ant hasn't, haven't

anzum handsome. "Me 'anzum" is a common expression like - "me luvver" or "me dear", all of which are used in S.Devon, Plymouth and Cornwall. These phrases are even used when addressing strangers - "Wat c'n I do ver ee, me anzum?" [What can I do for you, my handsome?]

apaze apace

a'perd halfpenny worth

apse a fastening on a door, window as hasp. "apse th' doar" [fasten the door] (1390)

arbs herbs

arely early

arg, argie-fy argue

arken harken, meaning "listen"

arrant errand - "gwain arrant" - "going on an errand". This was common phrase when I was a boy in Plymouth. "taakin' arrants" means to carry or deliver small parcels, goods (1750).

arrers arrows, harrows

arter after

atchett a hurdle hung across a stream to prevent cattle from wandering out of the field through which the stream flows. Also "rave".

ate eat. A grace which is said before meals runs as follows:
"Zum 'av mate an' they c'n ate,
Zum 'av mate an' can't.
But us 'av mate an' us c'n ate,
Zo let the Lourd be thanked."
[Some have meat and they can eat,
Some have meat and can't.
But we have meat and we can eat,
So let the Lord be thanked.]

ate'd eaten

ath'n hath not, has not

a-thurt, thert crosswise, [as "thwart" in a boat]. An obstruction such as a fallen tree would be "a-thurt th' raud" [Across the road].

aud old

aunt-sisters ancestors

aunsey to anticipate bad news

auver stayers over stairs - to go upstairs to bed - "tiz tam us wuz qwain auver stairs" [it is time we were going to bed].

a-veered afraid

a-vire on fire

avore before, until, or, "by the time that" (1750)

avore aul nevertheless, notwithstanding (1750)

avore days before daylight (1750)

avore me story I am digressing from my story

awiz always

awl hole

awm home

aw'mun of them

awp hope

aw's of us

awt of it - "I don't think nort awt" [I don't think nothing of it], meaning, "I am not impressed". Or it might be said, "I don't think nort to't".

ax ask - "Av ee ax'd un?" [Have you asked him?]

axen ashes (1750)

axpec expect

axwaddler an ash pedlar, one who dealt in, or collected, wood or peat ash. Before soap was in common use, ashes were placed in a strainer and water thrown onto them, which when poured off, was strongly alkaline. This liquor was called "lie" and used for washing clothes. The axwaddlers would go around the farmhouses collecting ashes and transporting them on pack horses. The ashes were rarely paid for in money, but were exchanged for drapery or other wares. The word survives in a number of Devonshire place names (1750).

ayer hair

azide beside

baastins beastings - the first milk after a calf is born, very rich and looked upon by some country people as very desirable for their own use.

baccy tobacco

back along some time ago

back'ouze scullery, room at the rear of the house in which various household chores were done.

backisvore reversed, back to front. Another word is "backends" with the same meaning.

bade bed

bain been

baint be not, am not

bair beer

baist beast

bait food - "baitin' th' 'osses" [feeding the horses]

bal a mine [Cornish]

ballin' or bawlin' shouting, calling, crying - a crying child would be said to be "ballin' ees eyes out" [crying his eyes out] ; a cow would be "ballin' for its calf"; a barking dog would be told to "stap yer ballin' "; "I ball'd tu'n" [I shouted at him].

ban' band

barriol barrel

baste-ees beasts, cattle

be are, is, am

be-dall'd bedevilled

beeve, baife beef

begger'd like "darned" or "blowed" - "I'll be begger'd if I doan't," meaning "I do" or "I will".

beller, bellow shout, call out loudly, cry, very similar to "ballin' " - "Thick aul effer, 'ers ballin' vit t'bust - 'ers bellowin' ver 'er caaff." [That old heifer - she is shouting fit to burst - she is calling for her calf.] "belvin" is a variation of the above.

better way should - "Us better way be makin' awm." [We should be going home.]

bevower before

biddle beetle; also the name of a thatching tool; the name of a large wooden mallet used for driving wedges into a tree trunk or baulk of timber in order to split it. The word biddle is applied to a number of different tools. *see* **vizgie**

bide stay, remain - "bide wer yu'm to." [stay where you are] ; "I'll let'n bide ver a bit." [I'll not do anything about it for a while.]

bigotive bigoted

bile-in' boiling

biler boiler - An old ex-sea captain uncle of mine said to me, after I had had a more than ample tea - "Yu'll bust yer biler, me nabs." [You will burst your boiler, my son.] Incidentally, he was in "sail" all his life, hated "steam" and after 40 years at sea, boasted that he had "never lost a ship nor a man." He was Cap'n Maynard of Bude, Cornwall and his schooner was *The Perseverance*. He also owned *The Independence* and *The Princess of Thule*.

billaziz bellows, a form of air pump made of wood and leather with a brass or iron outlet, which is put near a fire, air is pumped into the fire to make it blaze.

Billaziz

billy-o very much - " 'E laff'd lak billy-o." [He laughed a lot.] " 'E worked lak billy-o." [He worked very hard.]

bin been

birchen birch tree, made of birch wood

bissle to soil, make dirty - mother to child - "Daw'n ee bissle yersel!" [don't make yourself dirty.]

bist, [be'est] are - my grandmother would often ask - "Wer bist thee gwain?" [Where are you going?] (1750)

bit but

bit o' a tell a chat. *See* **tellin'**

biy boy

blade bleed

blaiged obliged

Bless vore to use a "charm" or "spell" to cure disorders such as warts, ring-worms, etc.

When I was a boy living in Exeter, I had an outbreak of ringworms on my neck, which would not clear up, despite the attention of doctor and clinic. My holidays were invariably spent on a farm at Whitstone on the Devon/Cornwall border near Bude, including the summer of 1924. My grandmother, who lived in a cottage near the farm, on seeing the ringworms on my neck said, "Granfer'l get rid aw'm ver ee - ee'l charm mun away."

Granfer instructed me to obtain some cold wood ash, which he took in the palm of his hand and then he stood behind me. I could not see what he was doing, but I believe he spat in the wood ash, at the same time reciting some sort of prayer or incantation. He then rubbed the wood ash onto my neck. Three days later there was no sign of my ever having ringworms! Local farmers would drive calves (prone to ringworms), to Granfer's cottage gate, where he would charm away the ringworms on the calves' backs. I was told that Granfer was the seventh son of a seventh son - this was apparently of great significance.

Incidentally, my Grandma used to prepare herbal medicants for various ailments and supply them to folk in the neighbourhood. Neither would accept any sort of reward.

This "blessing vore", or charming, was not looked upon as being strange or "wisht" in any way - it was accepted as part of the fabric of country life. (1750)

blaw blow

blid blood

blimmer a mild swearing adjective. I remember a small boy in North Devon saying to another, who had annoyed him - "Yu blimmer, yu blimmer, yu blimmer!" It could be applied to a horse who would not pull, a plough that had broken, in fact, anything or person causing annoyance.

blish blush

boddle bottle - "ot watter boddle" [hot water bottle]

boft bought

boogle bugle

botch a sore, boil, skin eruption, a mess. No doubt where our modern word "botch" [to make a mess of or to execute badly], originated. (1750)

boughten cakes or bread purchased from a baker's shop as opposed to those made at home. This form of adjective was common in the West country.

'bout about

braave brave, worthy, admirable

brack flaw

braid bread

brandies or brandis a four-legged stand used in the open fireplace like a "trivet", but larger, probably standing about 15 in high and 2ft long by about 1ft wide. The top is open.

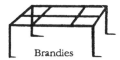

Brandies

Another version is "brandires" which translated means "burning stick irons" - a "brand" being a piece of burning wood, "ires" being irons.

brath broth [rhymes with "laugh"]

brawk broke or broken. *See* **scat**

brexis breakfast

brimmles, brimbles brambles, ie. blackberry bush;
"brimble" - one long runner.
A long "brimble" was used to catch rabbits. All the "preckels" [prickles] were removed except for about 3 in or 4 in at the tip or thin end. The "brimble" was then fed down a rabbit hole, being shaken up and down and twisted at the same time to make it thread down the hole. When it would go no further, a few more twists were given. If the "brimble" had come to a stop against a rabbit, extra twisting would cause the "preckels" to twist into its fur. The rabbit could then be pulled out into the open. One could tell if there was a rabbit within "brimble" reach by holding the back of the hand to the mouth of the hole. The heat from the rabbit could be felt.

brish brush, broom

britches breeches or "burches" [r.r.]

broft brought

browse brushwood, light coppice, undergrowth, cuttings from a hedge before being made into faggots.

bruk broke

budd'n button, also sheep or rabbit droppings. The burrs of the herb Burdock - "Cuckold Budd'nns". (1750)

bullicks bullocks [castrated bulls], a mature bullock is a "steer".

bulls bells

bul-yerds or billerds billiards

burd bread [r.r.]

burge bridge [r.r.]

Burton Briton [r.r.]

buster something difficult to cope with, one who is not easily beaten, one who excels.

caan't call'n awn can't call him home meaning can't remember him or it, variation would be "can't call 'ee awm" [I don't remember you].

cannle candle

Cap'n Captain - of a ship, but the managers of Cornish mines were also called "captains". "Cap'n o' Bal" [Captain (or manager) of the mine.] *See* **Bal**

carr' carry

carr'yer carrier

catch store, probably from "cache"

cauch something of little value - mother to child who had bought some nasty sticky sweets - "Wad'ee wanna buy thicky aud cauch ver?" [What did you want to buy that rubbish for?] Originally this word meant a medicinal preparation, a "slop" given to a sick person, or some unpleasant tasting physic. (1750)

cauchy left handed, "cack handed" elsewhere in Britain, but obviously with the same origins.

"Chaip-Jack" "Cheap-Jack", a market trader, stall-holder at a fair.

champeen champion

cheel child

chillern children

cheemed chimed

cherry-gobs cherry stones. When I was a lad in Plymouth, we used to buy "gob stoppers", large spherical hard, long lasting sweets, which when sucked, changed colour as the size diminished.

chicky cheeky, meaning disrespectful - "chicky varmint" [disrespectful rascal]

chimley chimney

chimley swape chimney sweep. People who did their own chimney sweeping would use a "vuz" [furze] bush on a piece of rope. This would be weighted and let down from the top of the chimney and pulled up and down.

chip to jolly or joke with, to poke fun.

chipples spring onions, also "scallions"

chittlin's chitterlins - edible pig's intestines, first cleaned, boiled and then either fried or eaten cold, sometimes soaked in vinegar.

chountin' nagging, taunting, scornfully reviling (1750)

chucked choked - "dry jist chucked [dry just choked] "chucked jist vule" [choked just full] - filled to capacity, especially after a hearty meal. "Th' draane's chucked.." [The drain is blocked.] (1750)

clain clean

clammer a footbridge - examples made of stone are found on Dartmoor.

claws, clawves, cloze clothes

climmey climb

cloam earthenware or clay - cloam jug, "cloam omm" [cloam oven]. These ovens were set in the side of the open fireplace and were used for baking. A wood faggot was burned in the oven and the ashes raked out, then a feather, or cloth duster, on a pole was dampened and used to remove the dust, (or most of it!). The food was then pushed into the oven and a flat stone, shaped to fit the opening, was used to seal the oven. This stone was made tight with dampened rags, moss or clay. A "modernisation" of this was the iron door hinges. The writer has had many a meal from such an oven and the memory lingers still. Pasties, tarts, cakes, biscuits - all were cooked to perfection in a cloam oven.

clomen made of clay (1750)

clurk clerk

co-at coat - pronounced "caw-at"

cob building material made of mud, cows' hair and straw [in S.W. Cornwall this is called "clob"]

cob a sturdy working pony of about 12 hands

comical constichiments chemical constituents [m.]

continny continue

coor'd cured

coose coarse - "coose mouthid" [coarse mouthed] ie. given to swearing.

cornder, coander a corner. Another peculiarity of the dialect is to sometimes include "d" in the middle of a word - "tailder" [tailor] (1750).

Cornish compliment a gift of no great value - "Yer yu be, yu c'n 'av this yer bit o' pasty, cuz I can't ate no more." [Here you are, you can have this piece of pasty, because I cannot eat any more.]

cotter a cottager

crabbid of acid disposition

crackin' chatting - "avin' a crack" [having a chat] "crackin' on" - talking at length, complaining, boosting - "Ers a wiz crackin' on 'bout zummat." [She is always complaining about something.]

crame cream
My auntie Bea told a tale about a bowl of cream at a certain tea party, which took place at Clawton, near Holsworthy [Hosery]. My grandmother, who was the village school teacher, had six daughters of marriageable age and four sons. It was felt that it would be a good idea to invite the curate of a neighbouring parish to tea as this might lead to a marriage in the family. My father, then about 8 or 9 years old, was admonished to be on his best behaviour and help to impress the curate that he was in the house of a family who knew "what was what", and could speak English, as opposed to the very broad local dialect.
At the tea table, my father, who had been told to "keep quiet", got on with the business at hand. His attention was drawn to the bowl of cream, where a wasp had got itself "stogged" down. My father watched it for a while in silence, but could at last no longer contain himself - he loudly called to his mother, "Yer Mater, ther's a waasp een th' crame - 'elp'n out aw't will ee?". No, none of my aunts married a curate.
Incidentally, it is impossible to get a cream nowadays with the flavour of the cream of my youth. The milk was put into a large pan, like one used for preserving, and allowed to stand for

about 12 hours in the dairy, usually a room leading off from the farmhouse kitchen. When the pan of milk was ready, the cream having risen to the top, it would then be placed very carefully on glowing wood embers, which had been raked forward onto the hearth of the open fire, making a hot pad about 4 in deep. Experience told the farmer's wife how much heat was needed and the right amount of embers required to attain the heat.

The milk slowly heated and in so doing, the cream on the surface formed into a crust, or "clotted". The aroma of the wood smoke was absorbed by the cream as it formed and it was this that gave the cream its marvellous flavour. How I wish I could once again taste cream made by this method. Modern clotted cream is good, but it just lacks that special flavour.

When the cream was fully clotted, the pan was removed and allowed to cool in the dairy. When completely cold the cream had formed into a firm crust, which was skimmed off with a cream skimmer, and put into a large bowl.

Cream Skimmer

The remaining milk was used for drinking cold - beautifully sweet it was too, or fed to the calves and pigs. Years ago one could buy skimmed milk in the retail dairies in towns for 1½ d a pint. This is often what the poorer people used in their tea.

Another interesting sidelight on cream (and butter), was that the flavour was affected by what the cows were eating. My mother made butter and cream when she was a girl at Woodley Farm, Boyton, between Whitstone and Holsworthy, North Devon. She was able to tell from the flavour of the cream, or butter, on which part of the farm the cows had been grazing, even which field, because she knew where the wild herbs or fodder were growing. She could detect wild mint, wild garlic, clover, turnips, mangold, etc., in the flavour.

crams nonsence - "a passel o' awl crams" [a parcel (lot) of nonsense] meaning stupid activities. Jan Stewer, (A.J. Coles), wrote a book entitled *A Passel o' awl Crams.*

crass across

created cremated [m.]
- "Er bain't gwain be buried, ers gwain be created." [She is not going to be buried, she is going to be cremated.]

cricket three-legged stool used for milking - three legs, because no matter how uneven the floor might be, the stool stands firm. Great agility was sometimes needed when hand milking a cow of uncertain behaviour. If she decided she didn't like you and lashed out [cows kick sideways], the trick was to grab the bucket with one hand, the cricket with the other and at the same time, leap backwards without spilling the milk, or falling flat on your back in the cow's dung - no mean feat! It is interesting to speculate that the game of cricket may have originated with the early use of a three-legged stool as a wicket - the three stumps now representing the three legs.

The word "wicket" may have been an alternative to "cricket". In Durham a four- legged stool is a "cracket".

Cricket

Criss-nin Christening

crock a large pot made of cloam in which butter or meat would be salted down. Also made of iron with three legs, used for cooking, or boiling potatoes for pig feed. (1750)

Crocks

crook an iron hanger with ratchet teeth, on which to suspend pots in the open hearth. On these would hang a "hussey" for resting pans on, and a "vountin" [fountain], which was a large kettle with a horizontal pipe coming from the lower front, instead of a spout. At the end of the pipe was a brass tap.Other kettles [with spouts],were tipped forward for pouring with a "lazy maid" attached to the kettle handle. This had a forward projecting handle, which was pushed downwards when water was required.

Crook

crooked words unkind words, derogatory remarks

crookee to bend down. A variation is "ruckee"

crowd a violin (1750)

crowder a fiddler, violinist

Crying the Neck an ancient ceremony performed in the field when the harvest is complete. A "neck" of straw was twisted [elsewhere "straw dollies"] and kept until the next harvest. "Neck" and "Nitch" are synonomous.

cumm'd came

curdlies curleys - ie., curly kale

cussen cannot, could not

cuz because

daid dead

dairly dearly

dap slap - "I'll giv'ee dap roun' th' yer awl" [I'll give you a slap on your ear hole]

dapper lively, quickly

daps similarity of one person with another (1750)

darn an expression like "dash" - "Well I'll be darned". "Caw, darn me", "Darned if I bain't zwaatin' ", [Darned if I'm not sweating] meaning "I am sweating". "Darned" would be used in exactly the same way as "beggered".

darter daughter

dashels thistles [E. Devon - "doishels"]

datchin' thatching

dead waste burial ground, churchyard

dear lill' zaul dear little soul - a common term of endearment applied to little girls. When applied to older girls, it usually has undertones of sympathy in it. Similarly, "pawer awl zaul" [poor old soul], would convey sympathy for an older woman. For an old man, it would be - "pawer awl begger" - even though the person in question might be quite rich.

Deb'n, Dem Devon

Demshur Devonshire

ded did

dee die

deed died

deeve deaf (1750)

dessay dare say

dews 'arp A hay rake. This is a word from East Devon, paticularly around the East Budleigh area and is interesting because it illustrates how words can be misunderstood, or deliberately mispronounced.

Dew's 'arp

The drawing shows what a hay rake looks like. The long tines are somewhat like the strings of a harp, which to the farm worker [unfamiliar with the drawing room variety] could be "Jew's Harp". [in itself a corruption of "jaw's harp", because it is played against the teeth]. "Jew's Harp" has been turned into "dews 'arp" - a hay rake.

dezaive deceive

dezaitvul deceitful

dimmett, dimpsy twilight ["dumps" in Dorset] (1750)

dirt'n dirty it, make it dirty

dith'n doth not, does not

dish bowl - "dish o' tay", a phrase which still survives from the time when tea was drunk from bowls without handles, before saucers came into use.

divvurnce difference

doag dog

doff take off [used in the spinning industry, with the same meaning]

dough boys dumplings. Dough with chopped suet mixed into it, made into spheres about the size of a golf ball and cooked in a stew.

douse to put out a fire, water divining. As fires are usually put out with water there may be a connection between the two meanings.

douse dust - especially that from threshing

draave, draive drive

drang-way narrow passage, similar to "ope"

drap drop

drashels flails, used for threshing corn. Two pieces of stick joined with raw hide.

Drashels

drashin thrashing (1750)

dray draw. I have heard older folk, including my grandmother, say that they had had their "votee drayed" [photograph drawn (taken)].
To "dray'n vore" - to pull it out, or forward (1750)

dree three

dree chairs three cheers

dree weel barra hand barrow with three wheels.

Dree weel barra

drekly directly

drek-shins directions

drexil threshold, doorstep (1750)

dripmebit threepenny piece

drot or drottle throat

drue through

drumbledrane a drone or humble bee. *See* **apple-drane**.

dude done, did (1387)

dung manure

dunnaw don't know

durzen dare not

eddy-f'cation a cross between "edify" and "education"

ee you, an abbreviation of "thee"

een in

een tu into

ees yes

ees fie or ees fay certainly, without doubt, [probably from "yes faith"] (1750)

eet yet

effers heifers

ent or empt empty, to empty, is empty

er her - often "er" is used in a male connection, - "am'n er dood it eet?" [hasn't he done it yet?]

erbons ribbons [r.r.]

exercised in spirit bothered

fairings presents or food bought at a fair, such as gingerbread, sweetmeats, ribbons, china figures - many of the latter being made on the continent, but also in Staffordshire.

fan-tag in a "fan-tag" means to be upset, annoyed - *See* **stewer**

fath faith or "By my faith". A very common expression especially in N. Devon. *See* **ees fay**

'feared afraid

Filling-stines Philistines [m.]

fishy-ate officiate [m.] - "Passon ax'd ef I'd fishy-ate at th' rails. I tell'd'n I didd'n naw nort bout fishy-ate'n, but I zed I'd taake on an rin mun ver'n". [Parson asked me if I would officiate at the revels. I told him I did not know nothing (anything) about officiating, but I said I would undertake to run them for him.]

fitch polecat

flibberts pieces

frig meddle, mess about with, to handle incompetently

frit fright, frightened

frizzed brushed up.
A girl who had brushed her hair to make it stand up and appear abundant, might have said of her that - "Er ayer wuz awl frizzed up like a vuz bush." [Her hair was all brushed up like a gorse bush.]

furnt front [r.r.]

furny-toor furniture

gaate gate

gabey, gawkey a simpleton

gake to stare in a stupid or vacant manner

gakin feeling in the dark, trying to see in the dim light, searching

gaw go, could also mean "gone" - "Ers gaw" [He has gone.] See **ers**

gaw back go back, deteriorate, revert to nature, - "E did'n du no work on ees varm an' it ztarted tu gaw back." [He did not do any work on his farm and it started to go back.]

gawk to look or gaze stupidly, one who is silly, foolish or acting stupidly.

gee'd'n gave him

genst against, often used to mean "in preparation for", to provide against some eventuality.

gert great or big - "wackin' gert" [very big] "gert" and "big" often used together - "Yu'm a gert big vule" [You are a great big fool].

get gate

git awm get home, a much used expression - used as a prefix to a sentence, like "get along with you" - "Aw git awm yu, I bain't doin' nort ver nobody" [Oh get home you, I'm not doing nothing for nobody] - meaning "I am not going to help anyone".

glane glean, gather

go gone - "Er'v go church" [She (or he) has gone to church] - "Amn go mazed?" [Has he gone mad?]

Godsen' Godsend, blessing, good fortune

graj'ly gradually

grammer-tone gramaphone [m.]

grammer, gran'ma grandmother, also applied to any old woman. If she was not quite so old, she might be called "Ol' Mother ..." this sometimes had slightly derogatory undertones.

granfer grandfather ["Granfer Grigg" - a wood louse]

grawpin groping

grin green
There is a place at Whitstone near Holsworthy, which for years I knew as "grin len aen". I discovered in my teens, that the name of the spot was "Green Lane End" or the junction of Green Lane with the main road from Launceston to Bude.

gude ver-nort good for nothing, a waster

gurl girl, pronounced "gur-rol"

guze goose - "Tavistock Guzie Vare" [Tavistock Goose Fair]

gwain going

heft weight, heavy - to "heft" a thing means to weigh it. A man would "heft" something in his hand to gauge its weight. Also means "to throw".

hell to pour

hend to throw

hie eye

himperence impudence [m.]

hoppyzaite opposite

housen houses

hove threw

hullifant elephant

id'n'ee isn't he

inederzide behind

injin engine

innerds inwards, always used to refer to one's internal organs

iny any

ire iron, "bar ire" [bar of iron] a crowbar

itums items, meaning habits, sayings, remedies, idiosyncracies, nonsense

iver ever

ivery every

ivery wips-wile every now and then, occasionally

iz'zel himself

jidge judge

jingle a two-wheeled vehicle drawn by a pony or "cob". The seats are at each side, so that the passengers face each other. The jingle is entered from the back by means of a step and small door.

The driver usually sits on the right or offside.

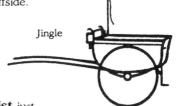

Jingle

jist just

jit jolt, poke - "I gid'n a jit een ribs" [I gave him a dig in the ribs]

jog-a-free geography [m.]

jonnick correct, honest

junket sweetened milk which has had rennet, [refined ox gall] added to it to make it curdle. Delicious - especially with clotted cream. It is the "curds and whey" of "Little Miss Muffet".

juty duty

kained, kaineed searched, looked around

kane keen

kape up keep up, meaning remain healthy, keep well

kapin' cump'my keeping company ie., courting

kay quay, key

kee cow. Pronounced "kae" or "kaeze" [cows] (1750)

kerping finding fault

kerrec correct

ketch or kitch catch

ketched or kitched caught - "ketched'n holt" [caught hold of him, or it]

kiss'n canst not, can't you

kittle kettle. My grandfather was very fond of "kittle brath", which comprised cubes of bread in a pudding basin, with about half a cupful of milk and half a cupful of hot water flavoured with salt and plenty of pepper. When he was a boy this was a common meal amongst the poor country people. Try it, you will be surprised how tasty it is. An alternative was to make it with all milk and sweeten to taste.

Kittle supported by "lazy maid"

kontry country

Kursmis Christmas [m.]

kuss curse

lace to give a thrashing, usually with something pliant, such as a leather strap, or a piece of rope, rather than with the fists.

laiz lies

laigs, ligs legs

launch launch [rhymes with "ranch"]. Will be heard in Plymouth, Devonport and district. A parallel is that the town, Launceston, is pronounced "Lansen". TV news readers please note.

lane lean

larn learn, teach - "I'll larn ee tu rade" [I'll teach you to read]

larrupin' beating, hard smacking - "Ev yu doant be'aave I'll giv'ee a gude larrupin' " [If you don't behave, I'll give you a good beating]

latch fancy, wish [to latch onto (modern) means to fasten onto another person or to understand a situation]

laver edible seaweed, usually fried

leery empty, a wagon without a load would "rin leery" [run empty]. A man who was hungry would "vale leery" [feel empty]

leff left

left leave, depart - " 'E idden no gude, I tull ee, 'twood be Godsen' if 'e wus to left th' parish". [He is'nt no good, I tell you, it would be a Godsend (blessing) if he was to leave the parish]

leggins leggings. Usually made of leather, but sometimes of canvas, worn around the calves and ankles, fastened by laces or studs which clipped into holes. They were oiled to repel water [as were boots], when worn for working. Those leggins reserved for going to market, or "Zindy-go-to-Matin" were highly polished.

Leggins

'lem eleven

lent loan - "gi'm th' lent o' me oss" [gave them the loan of my horse]

licker big - "prapper gert licker" [proper great licker] meaning very big

lidden tune or topic - "nine days' lidden" [nine days' wonder]

lie-a-bier lie abed

likky leek - "likky stoo" [leek stew], made with mutton, leeks and potatoes

lime or limeash floor cement floor. Lyme Regis in Dorset was a source of "bue lias" for cement making. Ships and barges came to Lyme to carry away vast quantities and at one time it was a thriving industry on that part of the coast.

limmer derogatory adjective applied to another person - like "blimmer"

linney linhay, where carts, wagons, tools and equipment are kept. Usually open along one side towards the farm yard, the other three sides being enclosed.

lissom active

live life

long tailed rabbit pheasant. This is an expression used by a person who, when out shooting rabbits, "accidentally" hits a pheasant when he "mistakes" it for a rabbit.

loo lee, shelter, the side away from the wind

"Lor massy" "Lord have mercy"

loss loose, mislay - "Doan't ee loss 'n" [Don't you loose it]

lostin' losing - "I didden mind lostin' me awl 'at, but me aid got wet". [I didn't mind losing my old hat, but my head got wet.]

lousterin' lowly, menial

lukee look - "lukee to'n" [look at him]

lukin' looking

lustree, lewstrey to bustle about. *See* **loustering** (1750)

luvver lover. "Me luvver" is a phrase used by both men and women, especially in and around Plymouth and Cornwall, even when talking to a stranger - as the Londoner will use "ducks" or "mate". Men address each other as "me luvver" as a matter of course. "Me dear" and "Me bootee" [beauty], are also used in the same manner and it sometimes leads to misunderstanding when a "vurriner" is so addressed.

maake'n spake make it speak - meaning make a sound with or play a musical instrument.

maakin' awm going home - "Tiz time us wuz maakin' awm" [It is time we were going home]

maakin' tracks "making tracks" means to leave footmarks in the ground. This is obviously done by walking and to walk one has first to make a start, so to "maak tracks" means "to go".

maake wise to pretend

maade'n to forced him

maid "Maid" usually meant a young girl or "lil maid" [little girl] whereas "maiden" referred to a teenage girl. In the country districts the word "maid" was not used to refer to a servant who, possibly working in the farmhouse, helping with the milking, making butter etc., would be called "th' 'elp" - " 'elpin' een th' 'ouse" [helping in the house]

maister master or employer although one farmer would address another as "maister". Can also be used to imply a large quantity, size, or to indicate quality - "maister vine bullicks", "maister long time", "maister gert vule".

maized, maazed mad, stupid -"Yu'm maized as a brish stick" [You are as stupid as a brush handle].
This reference to the stupidity of a brush handle is found in other parts of Britain. It is because a brush will only go where it is pushed?

mane men

mania-scrip manuscript [m.]

marr'd married

mate meet, meat *See* ate

maundering grumbling, muttering

maw intestines, variation "maw-guts"

Methody Praicher Methodist Preacher

mezel' myself

min,mun them, they. "Those" and "them" would never be used, it would always be "min", "mun" or "they". However, I have heard "thuze" as a polite version of "those" or "these".

mind remember, notion - "I can mind the tame ..." [I can remember the time ...] "I'm minded to ..." [I have the idea or notion to ...]

mite a little

mizzy-maazy the same as "maized", except that it could also be applied to an object or piece of equipment which is

not functioning properly.

mommet a dummy, an effigy, doll, scarecrow, often implying derision. This word has the variations of "moppet" and "poppet" with witchcraft connections.

mordle mortal

mort a lot, large amount, much

mote or moot the bole of a tree. When ground is cleared of coppice, the "motes" are kept for burning in the open hearth, with some earth still clinging to them. One or two of these make a fine, long-burning "back log".

mow a meadow, or to cut grass or corn

mulk milk

mulkee to milk

mump aided silly, like "addle aided"

murdy maakin' mischievous

muscrawl a caterpillar [E. Devon] "muzcraw" [N. Devon]

musicker musician

muxy dirty, muddy, deep mire, filthy

"My gar" an exclamation like "My goodness"

nack knock, is used in a common enquiry about health or welfare - "Ow be nackin' vore then?" [How are you knocking forward then?] or "How are you?"

naedle or niddle needle

nair near - also means tight-fisted, miserly, mean - "Ers za nair 'erd skin a vlint ver a penny an zpowel a zixpenny nive duin o't". [She is so mean she would try to take the skin off a flintstone for a penny and spoil a sixpenny knife doing of it.]

naith beneath

nap rise in a hill, horizon, top of a hill - "over th' nap o' th' ill, out o' zite." [Over the top of the hill, out of sight.]

narrer narrow

nat not

nawze knows, nose

naw'd knew

naw-tiz notice

neast near, close to

neether, nither neither

niddick neck

'nif and if

nich a large bundle of straw or reed used in thatching. The nitch is divided into smaller bundles, which are bound with rope made of a few twisted strands of reed and when complete are called "waads". Long "waads" go along the ridge of a roof, but are not seen when the thatching is completed.

Nitch

nitch notch

niver never

noan none

nort nothing

nubbies buns made with yeast and flavoured with saffron.

'nuff enough

obfuscation innebriation, drunkeness

ockerd awkward

odds difference, "no odds" means "no difference" or "no matter" or "not important" - "didd'n odds 'n" [did not care about it] or "it was a matter of indifference".

'oldin o't holding of it, meaning "keeping it to yourself", secretive.

'oller shout

'ollerdays holidays

'omley homely, meaning feeling at home, welcome, at ease.

omn oven

o'mun of them

on-cum-ferable uncomfortable

on upon engaged on doing, occupied - "Yer! Wat be yu on upon?" [Here! What are you doing?]

ood wood, rhymes with the Scottish "guid" [good]. A tool for cutting wood and saplings from a hedge is called a "ood 'ook" [wood hook].

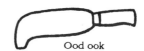
Ood ook

Faggots, bundles of hedge cuttings, would be stacked near the kitchen door in a "ood rick". Also written in dialect as "yude".

oozle whistle. "Wet yer oozle." [Have a drink.] An aunt of mine warned a country child not to stand too near the edge of the railway platform, because the train was coming. She received the answer, "Er am'n oozled eet!" [She has not whistled yet!]

ope a passage way between buildings, to open - "Ope th' doar, wu'llee?" [Open the door, will you?] Incidentally, "wull'ee" is synonomous with "please".

ordain intend

ordained planned, proposed

or'nery ordinary

ort anything. *See* **nort**

orted hurt. My mother used to tell of an old farm labourer who had fallen off a horse. She said to him, "Have you hurt yourself, Jan?" "Naw" he said, "I baint orted, but I'v tored me mouth and nacked me 'aid." ["No" he said, "I'm not hurt, but I've torn my mouth and knocked my head."]

orwiz always

oss horse

o't of it, pronounced "awt" - "I don't think nort o't" [I don't think nothing of it], meaning, "I am not very impressed." This could also be expressed - "I don't think nort tu't." [I don't think nothing to it.]

outdacious outrageous

Ow-dee-do? How do you do?

ow-zum-iver however

paice peace, piece

paice a piece of land given to a child so that the proceeds of tilling, rent or income would accrue to that child. Often the father, or grandfather, would till the land, sell the crop and credit the child with the income. I remember this practice on several farms in N. Devon. The name of the child would be given to the land or field, thus we come across such field names as "Jenny's Piece". The word "portion" was also used.

paice tellin' piece telling, meaning reciting. Children would "larn a paice" to be recited at Socials, parties or in Chapel.

paakin strolling, idling, parading, promenading

parr-is parish

pairt shrewd

pait peat

passel parcel, lot

pass'n parson

patickley particularly

pauss, poss post - "gaate poss" [gate post]

peek or pick two pronged fork used for "pitching" [throwing] sheaves when making a load on a wagon or a rick.

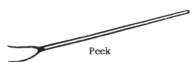

Peek

pegs pigs

pellum, pillom dust, especially that found in barns, tallet lofts, etc., of a cobwebby and straw nature, also spelt in old dialect "plim".

pennerd pennyworth

pernt print [r.r.]

pert part

pervection perfection

pewl pull

pewlin pulling

pickin' like "making tracks" - "Tiz time us wuz pickin' way awmwards." [It is time that we were going home.]

pinney raydin' penny reading. A penny was paid to enter the village hall to hear prose and poetry read. Sometimes there was also singing.

piskies or **pixies** fairies, usually inhabiting Dartmoor [Devon] or Bodmin Moor [Cornwall] but known to wander into any part of the two counties, when the whim takes them. Very good luck to see one, but if you do, be sure to be polite and in no way upset him - the consequences could be a little unpleasant - your milk might curdle or your hens stop laying. In fact, you can never tell what might happen - so be warned!
In some parts of the U.S.A. to be "pixilated" means to act foolishly, be a bit mentally unbalanced.

pitch throw

planch, plancheen plank, board, floor, made of "planches" [French - *planche*].

plat plot. Usually a small area of ground adjacent to the house. *See* **ricks-plat**

poachin' to trample by cattle so as to cut up the ground and make it muddy. A "poached" field would be one where the cattle had been turned into it too often, resulting in a "stoggy" state with "zugs" - little islands, about the size of a bucket, of grass and rushes.

pook haycock. A pile of hay in the field after it has been "tredded", [turned], awaiting collection to be made into a rick. (1750)

popple pebble, hence the name of the village Newton Poppleford, on the river Otter, E. Devon.

popple-stones pebbles [Anglo-Saxon *papol-stan*]

prapper proper, good or fine. Used in conjunction with "job", which in this case does not mean "employment", but "situation", "development", "accomplishment". "A prapper job" means that "it is very satisfactory".

praich preach

previous early

prong four-pronged long-handled hay fork, also used for straw and "mucking out" stables and shippons.

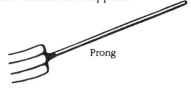

Prong

pun tap up on top

purt, purty pretty [r.r.]
"purt nare" [pretty near] meaning almost

put about puzzled, disconcerted, annoyed

put vore to go out with, to set off

quane queen

quayer queer, choir

quay-it quiet

quayt quite

quid o' baccy piece of chewing

tobacco, or a piece of compressed tobacco which is cut into pieces. Sailors would soak tobacco leaves in molasses and sew them into canvas to mature. This tobacco was known as "spun yarn", a name derived from the thread used to sew the canvas. It could be used for smoking or chewing. The bundle of tobacco in the canvas was called a "prick" of tobacco.

Prick of baccy

rabbert rabbit.
The story is told of the Devonshire poacher who became a soldier in the 1914-18 war. His C.O. happened to be a magistrate well-known to the poacher. The C.O. addressed his men about going to France and what they might expect when they got there. He finished by asking the men if they had any questions. The poacher spoke up saying, "This yer France us is gwain tu, Zur, be it rabberty kontry be iny chance?"

raed, road reed, combed straw used for thatching. "Rishes" [rushes], also called "reed" were used for thatching ricks. There is another type of reed known as Norfolk reed, very little of which is grown in the Westcountry. It has a longer life on a roof than straw.

raich reach

raid read, reed, red *See* **erd**

rail revel, a fete or garden party

rail real

raimid stretched

raizin reason

raipers reapers

rasselin' wrestling

rat rot

ratted rotted

rate right. Any word ending with "ight" would be pronounced thus.

raud road, rode

raw row

raw tiddy vry raw potato fry.
Sliced raw potatoes, bacon pieces, onion, milk and water, pepper and salt in a covered frying pan. Simmered until cooked, approximately half an hour. Delicious!

rawze rise, rose

rayfoozul refusal

raymes framework

raytrait retreat

regler regular

reppy-tation reputation

rick stack of hay, corn, faggots

ricks-plat an area of ground near the farm buildings where the corn ricks were built.

Staddle stone

The stone mushrooms, used now as garden ornaments, were sited in the "ricks-plat" and were used to keep the rick raised above the ground.

rimlets remnants, little pieces

rin run

rin word "run word" means to break one's word or promise

rishes rushes ."Ricks" were "datched" with "rishes".

rissel rustle

rist rust **riz** rise, raise - past tense: "riz'd" - "Er brade a'm riz'd eet." [Her bread (dough) has not risen yet]

roiley to rail [Exmoor]

rote memory, one learnt poetry by "rote"

rowcast rough cast, plastering mud onto a wall by throwing. *See* **scat.** Also to abuse, accuse, hence "to throw mud".

rowl fair, level [Exmoor]

rucksel noise, disturbance

rummage rubbish, nonsense, junk, odds and ends, silly talk. This word was in use in the time of Sir Francis Drake. It was used by seamen when talking about ballast and any other rubbish to be thrown away when "rummaging" or cleaning out, the ship. The ballast got a bit smelly after a few months and would be changed, this was called "rimmaging" the ballast.

Saltash rig an expression heard in Plymouth and district to indicate that the enterprise has been unsuccessful and is summed up as "a wet arse and no fish".

sar serve

sar'd served

sassy saucy, meaning impudent, disrespectful, high spirited; a lively high stepping horse could be "sassy" or a "maiden with an eye for the lads" could be called a "sassy baggage".

saujer soldier - "gwain ver a saujer" means intending to "join up"

savise sense, to understand

scat broken, break, throw - "the cloam jug be scat" [the earthenware jug is broken]. "Er'v scat ees aul 'at een th' river." [He has thrown his old hat in the river.]

scollard scholar

scrall crawl - [rhymes with "pal"]. A small child - "lill scraller".

scritch screech, scream, cry

scummer upset, dissention, controversy

shammel mate shambles meat. Meat "boughten" from a butcher as opposed to that produced on the farm for home consumption. The area of the town where the butchers had their stalls or shops was called the "shambles". [See remarks about Butchers Row, Exeter, page 7.]
When an animal was killed for home consumption, not all of it could be eaten at once, consequently a large part of it was "salted down" to preserve it.

shape sheep

sharps shafts of a waggon, cart or trap

shayves sheaves

shet shut, shoot.
An uncle of mine speaking of a town dog

which had been worrying his sheep, said, "I'll shet they aud doag." [I will shoot that old dog.] "They" is very often used in place of "that".

shevvers small pieces

shh this is not so much a word as a sound of assent or agreement. The sound is made by shaping the lips as for "sugar" *but*, and this is important to the meaning, the breath is drawn *in* sharply. The use of this sound is common in North Devon and throughout Cornwall, and is used to signify "I agree", "Yes", "That is right", etc.

shippin shippon - a cattle shed where milking is done and where cattle are kept during hard weather. Originally "sheep pen".

shoeg this word repeated a number of times, [the first "shoeg" being long and those following called more quickly], was a common way of calling pigs. Cows were called by "Oi, oi, oi ..."
When weaning a calf to take milk from a bucket by allowing it to suck one's fingers held below the surface of the milk, one would encourage it by saying quietly, "sug, sug, sug ..."
When throwing out grain for chickens, one called, "Chook, chook, chook ..."

shords, shards sherds, pieces of broken china or pottery. An aunt of mine would hammer into small fragments a broken plate or cup and throw the tiny pieces to the chickens to peck. These and small stones act as "teeth" for a chicken, which has none, who takes them to grind up food. My aunt called these small pieces of china "shards".

shore 'nuv [or 'nuff] sure enough

A common phrase of agreement is "Oh ace yu, shore nuff." - often followed by "shh".

short commons poverty, lack of food

showel, shoel shovel - "They put'n t'bade wi' a showel", means they buried him.

Showel

sissin' hissing

sive scythe

sivver several

skammel scramble

skatt a shower of rain. Risden quotes a proverb: "When Hall-down [Haldon Hill, near Exeter], has a Hat, let Kenton beware of a skatt". Kenton is a pretty village, between Exeter and Dawlish, which has a lovely 14th century church.

skawer score

skiver skewer

skillet a saucepan, usually made of gun metal, with a handle. Three legs protruded from the bottom, two opposite the handle and one longer one below it. This had the effect of making the handle incline upwards, so that when the skillet was standing in the hot embers of an open fire, the handle was at the correct angle for holding - bearing in mind that the fire was just above ground level.

I have a skillet which my grandmother used.

Skillet

skriddick morsel

skuil, skauwl, skuel school. "Skuil maister" [School master].

slammick, slummick to shamble, to be untidy, to walk in a sluggish manner.

smarless smallest

smitch smeech, a dirty smoke from a fire. An oil lamp with its wick turned up too high would emit a black smoke, which would be a "smitch". If the wind was in the wrong direction and blowing the smoke down the chimney, the kitchen would be said to be "vule a smitch" [full of smoke].
If a dirty deposit from a bonfire got onto the clean washing hanging on the line, the housewife would complain that there was "a dirty aul smitch on me claws." [A dirty old smoke on my clothes]

s'naw dost though know? Or, do you know? The "s" in front of a word always indicates the abreviation of "dost" or "dost thou". Heard more in Somerset nowadays than in Devon.

snaw driff snowdrift

spake speak, talk - "I'v yerd er spake awt" [I have heard her talk about it] "I'v yerd a spake aut" [I have heard it spoken of.]

spar a piece of split hazelwood, roughly the thickness of one's little finger, about three feet long, sharpened at both ends, then twisted and bent so that one arm is a little longer than the other, but parallel. The spar is used by the thatcher to keep in place the "waads" of reed, which go to make up the roof. In N. Devon and Cornwall is sometimes called a "spear".

Spar

spark court - to "gaw sparkin' " means "to go courting" - "Ees sparkin' thick maiden o' Varmer Jordan's" [He is courting Farmer Jordan's daughter].

sparticles spectacles

spich speech

spickety spotty - "spickety vaaced" [spotty faced]

spinney-jinney a spinning wheel; "spinney jinney" is a corruption of "Spinning Jenny", which is a mule spinning frame invented by Arkwright and said to be named after his daughter, Jenny.

splits small, unsweetened bread buns, made with yeast, eaten with jam and cream. This is the true Westcountry split. The introduction of the "scone" by "vurriners" in recent years, is to be deplored, because the split is the *right* complement to real clotted cream and jam. "Splits" are known in Plymouth and district as "tough cakes" and in other parts of Devon and Cornwall as "cut rounds". Visitors please accept no substitute!

spo-as suppose

spowel spoil

spranked splashed, sprinkled, splattered

spreader a bar, usually made of wood with metal attachments, used to keep apart the traces of the horses. Also called "swivvle trees".

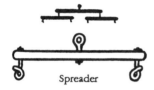

Spreader

squab young pigeon - "squab pie" is a Westcountry delicacy.

squale squeal

stag a cock

stame steam

stap stop, step

stappin' up staps stepping up steps, meaning going up stairs, or working a treadmill for raising water, grinding corn, or as punishment in prison.

stauld stole, stolen

stay sty

steev'd stiff - "steev'd wi' cau'd" [frozen with the cold] .Often coupled with "yarky", also meaning very cold, inclement or damp, "steev'd and yarky".

stoanen made of stone

stogged bogged. Land which is wet and in need of draining, is said to be "stoggy". A person or vehicle sunk into the mud and unable to move is "stogged".

stoo stew

stooer a fuss, creating a dust, getting upset, bothered, creating trouble. "Doan ee git yersel een a stooer" [Don't get yourself upset] "Mind wot yu'm duin way thicky brish - yu'm maakin' awful stooer way'n." [Mind what you are doing with that brush - you are making an awful dust with it.]

stook several sheaves standing in the field, with their heads of grain uppermost, leaning against each other to dry before being built into a rick, or stored in a barn, prior to thrashing.

Stook

straakin' straggling

strapper an unskilled person, an odd-job man, often applied to someone who undertakes a job for which he is not qualified, and ends up making a mess of it.

strick strike. An old man whom I knew when speaking of his grandfather clock said, "Ivery time 'e stricked 'e sissed lak an aul snaake." [Every time it struck it hissed like an old snake.]

strikes loads

stroil spoil

stude stood

stummick stomach

suiant, sueant presentable, in keeping with, admirable, correct

swart sharp, cutting - could be applied to the weather or a person's tongue. Also has "black" connotations, hence "swarthy". (1216)

taaste taste - "Ivery wan tu ees taaste as th'aul ooman zayd wen er kissed th'osses nawze." [Everyone to his taste, as the old woman said when she kissed the horse's nose.] There is a less polite version which refers to the other end of the horse.

tack to smack. *See* **dap**

tacker small boy, always referred to as a "lill tacker" [little boy].

taich teach

Taildors Niddles Tailors' needles - a weed.

'tain contain, obtain

tallet loft. The "tallet loft" usually over the stable, but could be on the first floor of any farm building, in which hay, grain or any dry fodder could be stored.

The floor could be used for threshing corn with flails and for winnowing. There was always a door opening out above ground, through which sheaves could be pitched from a wagon standing below. There would be a beam above the door projecting outwards on which was a pulley to take a rope for hoisting or lowering sacks.

"Tallet" probably comes from "Tally" meaning to count or keep a record.

tamp dampen or press down ["tampt" past tense] - "Us tampt down th' vire genst gwain bade." [We made the fire safe in preparation for going to bed.] Ashes would be heaped upon the fire to "tamp" it down, so that it would smoulder all night. When the fire was disturbed next morning and blown with the "billaziz" [bellows], it would blaze up again. A man would also "tamp" down the "baccy" in his pipe prior to lighting it.

tannin *see* **larrupin'**

taps 'n tail head over heels

tarl at all, tall

tarnal eternal

tart everyone knows what a tart is, but in most other parts of the country, it is usually a "sweet". In the Westcountry tarts have a far greater variety. They have pastry top and bottom, to make them more easily eaten with the hands in the field, and can have any sort of filling, especially of a savoury nature, such as turnip and mutton, egg and bacon, "tiddy an' mate", parsley, egg and cream, in fact, anything which might be available and in any combination.

Sweet tarts were usually apple, apple and blackberry, or apple and wortleberry. Tarts were usually eaten cold, because the "bake" in the "cloam omn" would be once, or possibly twice, a week. A Westcountry man is unlikely to eat hot apple tart, in fact he would probably spurn it, the cream would melt and that would never do! Personally, I would not thank you for hot apple tart. Ugh!

taw-ud toad. A difficult person would

be referred to as a "praaper aul tawud". A naughty child would be told, "Yu'm a praaper lill tawud".

tay tea; "try to maak a tay" means "do have a good tea" or "eat as much as you can".
Tea, first used in England in 1601, according to the Oxford Dictionary, was then spelled "tee" and pronounced "tay".

tayjisness tediousness

tear, tare hurry, bustle, be annoyed - "Ers een a prapper aul tare." [She is very annoyed.]

telegraap telegraph
"telegraap way-ers" [telegraph wires]

tell'd, tull'ed told, spoke about

tellin' speaking, talking about - "Us wuz tellin' 'bout 'e on'y t'other day." [We were talking about him only a few days ago.]

tull tell

tull'ee tell you

tervee struggle to get free. *See* **towzee**, the two together give "towzee tervee" [topsy turvy].

thafe thief

thave thieve ["th' " as in thine]

thaise, thoose these

they them, those, that.
See **shet**, where "they" is used for "that"

thicky this. A variation is "thicker", usually meaning "that". An abbreviation of both is "thick", the "th" is pronounced as in "thine". Used in Cornwall, Devon, Dorset and Somerset. "Theck" or "thec-

kee" from the Anglo-Saxon "thyllice" or "thylce", Scottish "thilk".

thit that

thoft thought

thunk thought ["th" as in "thine"]

thurdle-gutted thin, of starved appearance

thurzel's "theirselves" meaning "themselves"

tidden it is not

tiddy, teddy potato - "tiddy an' mate pasty"; [potato and meat pasty]. In Cornwall, pasties are known as "tiddy-oggies". In the Navy, a man from Cornwall is often called an "oggie", or is nicknamed "Oggie".

Pasty

tiddyvate titivate, bedeck, adorn

till to sow the seed, to cultivate

timbern timbered, made of wood

tinner tenor

titch, tetch touch

to The use of "to" is often mystifying to "vurriners", [especially, it seems, to some actors trying to imitate the dialect]. The word is frequently tacked onto the end of a sentence relating to places or positions - "Wer's it to?" [Where is it?] "Wer be gwain to?" [Where are you going?] "Wer'v'ee put'n to?" [Where have you put it?] and so on. However, it could be used as follows: "Bide wer yu'm to" [Stay where you are] or "Laiv'n wer ees to" [Leave it where it is]. Other uses are - "Oh ace, 'e lives over to Upcott", and "Th' way it wuz to ..." meaning "The circumstances were ..."

t'ome to home, meaning "at home", or on a visit to one's parental home. Could also be expressed as, "'ome-'bout" [home-about].

tooked agin'n opposed to it, a disliking for

torn, tourn the wheel of a spinning wheel, the whole thing being a "quill torn" or "spinning torn".

towan downland, usually on the coast [Cornish]

towzee toss, tumble

trait treat. "Zindy Skuel Trait" - [Sunday School Treat] - the annual trip to the seaside, where the children paddled, consumed "hokey cokey" [ice cream], and drank fizzy lemonade from a glass bottle with a glass marble in the neck. Mothers would take their market baskets filled with pasties, tarts, cream, seedy cake and saffron "nubbies".
Sometimes a schoolroom, or church hall would be borrowed and in this the meals would be laid out from the over-flowing baskets.

traade trade. Usually applied to some product, or food, which is considered to be of no great value, or is unfamiliar. A farmer given food to which he is not accustomed, would say, "Wad'ee call this yer aul traade then?" [What do you call this unusual food?] meaning "How dare you serve me with food to which I am not accustomed - I don't like the look of it and I am not inclined to eat it!"

traipsin' walking, usually in a tired or bored manner - "traipsin' roun' th' shaps" [walking around the shops]. This word is derived from "trapes" [a slut, trollop or one who was slovenly, idle or "walked the streets"].

trap light, two-wheeled, one-horse vehicle, used for passengers or light goods.

trigged up dressed up

trivet a three-legged stand, which is placed in the glowing embers of an open fire, on which to stand pots or pans. The top is open.

Trivet

trow trough

truck similar to "cauch" and "crams". Also means dealing, trading - "Wudden av no truck way'n" [Would have nothing to do with him].

tuck shorten, shrink. After cloth had been woven, it was fulled [with Fuller's Earth] or "tucked". The cloth was beaten in water of a soapy nature causing it to become compact. Exeter has its Hall of "The Company of Tuckers, Dyers and Shearsmen". The surname Tucker is derived from this trade, as are place names such as "Tuckingfield", a place where there had once been a fulling mill.

tuke on took on, meaning to become employed, or engaged, in some activity. One man might say that he had "tuke on" to be employed as a waggoner, or another that he had "tuke on" to become a parish councillor. A woman might say that she had "tuke on" to run a stall at the jumble sale.

tummull tumble

turmits turnips

turn over a woollen shawl

turtleshell tortoise shell [m.]

'twad'n it wasn't

ulse else

umbye by and by

umman woman [pronounced "oomun"]

underd hundred [r.r.]

unger'd hungry - "Be ee unger'd Jan?" [Are you hungry John?]

uny, iny any

upperds upwards

upzot upset

upztore an upset, controversy, disagreement, similar to "stooer".

ur or

urch rich [r.r.]

urd rid [r.r.] - "got urds o'n" [got rid of it]

urgeement regiment [r.r.]

us we

us 'ud we would

us 'uv we have

us be we are

us is we are

us'll we will

us better way we should

uv of

vaace face

vaeld field

vailin feeling

vair fair, fare

vaith or vath faith

vaityers features

val-de-dals fol-de-rols

vall fall [rhymes with "pal"]

vall'd fell

vam-lee family

vard'n farthing [$1/4$ of an old penny]

varmint rascal, vermin

vate or **vit** feet

Vather Kersmis Father Christmas [r.r.]

vears piglets, a N. Devon word

veared afraid, frightened

veed feed

vefty fifty

venn fen, marshy ground

vergit forget

vew few, view [pronounced "voo", with a slight "e" sound in the first "o"]

viddle fiddle, violin

viddy or vitty fitting, proper, well-made, correct, acceptable, etc.

viggy pud'n fig pudding

vile file

vine fine

vittles, viddles victuals, food

vive five

vizgie a double-bladed digging tool. One [horizontal] blade is for digging earth and the other, [vertical], opposite the first, is in the shape of an elongated axe head and used for cutting the roots of trees when removing "motes" from the ground which is being cleared. There is a Cornish story, in which the word is spelt "phiskey", of a man who wished to sell his wife. This was a fairly common practice, many people errone-ously thinking it to be legal to sell a wife. The wives did not seem to object. The man in question offered his wife for sale and the only bid he received was to exchange her for a "phiskey", but as the husband already had one, no deal was concluded.

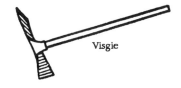

Visgie

Around Exeter and East Devon, the tool is called a "two bill", on Exmoor it is a "two bydle", in Somerset it is a "bisgey" and the French word is "*besague*".

vinger finger

vinnied mouldy, mildewed, spotted with mould. Dorset cheese is "Blue vinnied". In old writings spelled vari-ously as "vinew'd", "vinnewed", "finew'd", "fenowed", "fenowned", "fenne", "whinid" [Shakespeare].

vire lock fire lock - a gun

virkin firkin, a small barrel, which could be any size, not necessarily the correct firkin measure, which is much larger than a "virkin". The "virkin" was used to carry cider into the fields whilst hay-making or harvesting. It would be covered with dock leaves and put in the shade in the hedge to keep it cool. The size of a "virkin" was usually about 9in to 12 in long and about 7 in to 8 in in diameter and carried with a leather thong.

Virkin

Bottles of cold tea, without milk or sugar, were also taken and pushed down a rabbit hole to keep cool. Very refresh-ing too, is cold tea, and you don't have to sleep it off !

vlee fly

vlid flood

vlower flour, flower

vlower or vluer floor

voaks, vokes folks, people

main vokes men folk

ummeen voke women folk

voller, volley follow

vollier follower, one who followed after a girl. Servants of the gentry were warned that "followers" would not be tolerated.

voocher future

vore fore, front, main. Sometimes used to indicate going forward, or moving in front of. "Gwain vore th' raud" [going along the road], "laidin' th' vore oss" - leading the front horse when it was hitched to the shafts of a waggon, to help the horse between the shafts, to pull a load up across a harvest field to the road, where the "vore oss" would be unhitched and taken back to help with the next load. "Laidin' th' vore oss" was usually the job of a boy who, having unhitched, would clamber up onto the broad back of the "shire" and ride back for the next load. There was no saddle - one sat on a sack and I have painful memories of doing this task all day. The insides of my legs were almost raw, caused by the sweat from the horse and the roughness of the sack. The word "fore" is used also to indicate "main". Thus we find many townships in the Westcountry with the main street called "Fore Street".

vore-numes forenoons, mid-morning snack. Also "lemzes" [elevenses], "lunch", "nunch".

vore zunded fore sunned meaning facing the sun, or on the sunny side.

vor for (1220)

vor'n for him

vorrard forward

vorrid forehead, or the edge of a field

vort-nit fortnight

vorty forty

vot fault - "vinden' vot" [finding fault]

vountin fountain. *See* **crook**.

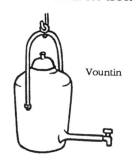

Vountin

vower flour

vrash fresh

vrens friends

vrim from

vrit fright, frightened

vool, vouel fool, full, fill

vule o' bumption full of bumptiousness, boastful, "puffed up".

vuller'd a fellow had

vurder further

vurriner foreigner

vury purty aitin' very pretty eating, meaning tasty, good food.

vussled hurried, fussed

vuzlin', vustlin' fussing

vust first - "verst" in 1387

vute foot

vuz furze, gorse. An untidy person would be said to look as though he had been "pulled drue a vuz bush backerds" [pulled through a furze bush backwards].

A town or village claiming superiority over a rival would say it was a "busy town" when the other was a "vuzzy down" - "Kirton [Crediton] was a busy town when Exeter was a vuzzy down." Obviously incorrect, but showing the pride of the inhabitants of Crediton in their town, which, incidentally, was the seat of the Bishopric before it moved to Exeter over 800 years ago.

waad a bundle of straw, or reed, used in thatching. *See* **nitch.**

Waad

waap, wop to beat, to strike, a blow. Used in America. The boxer, Cassius Clay [Mohammed Ali] was heard to say that he was going to "wup" his opponent. In 1750 the word was "whappet", later shortened to "whap".

wad'ee want what did you want, also meaning "why"

wadden wasn't

waik week, weak

wain when

wain waggon

wait, wets wheat - "vaeld o' wets" [field of wheat]

walk tu Exter means difficulty in reading, or "it is as difficult for me to read as it is to walk to Exeter".

wale wheel

wan one

wance once

wan other one another

wan an t'other one and the other

want a mole, small burrowing animal. Common word in E. Devon. (1750)

warrner warrant, guarantee - sometimes a lawyer or solicitor was called a "warmer".

wayin within

way'n with him

weel will

weend wind

wee, wi' or way with

went gone. "Ded orter a went" [did ought to have gone], meaning should have gone.
"Er'v went" [she's gone], or could be, "Er'v go".

weppins weapons

wert, whort whortleberry, bilberry, blueberry

whortin' to go picking whortleberries. Whort and apple is the most marvellous combination, with a "whackin gurt dob a' crame on't". The Westcountryman usually prefers his pie served with the crust upside down in the dish first and then the "innerds" of the pie placed on top with the cream to crown it.

wips-wile occasionally, now and then

"Wish'ee well" very common expression meaning "I wish you well" or as we would say today, "Goodbye" - which originally meant, "God be with you". If one wants to be jocular, one says, "Wish ee well ver now, but I'll zee ee agin vore then", meaning "Goodbye until I see you next time, but I'll see you again before then".

wisht unhappy, unhealthy, pale-faced, strange - "Er wuz lukin' a mite wisht wen I zeed er" [She was looking a little unwell when I saw her]. "I wood'n gaw tu thick 'ouse arter dark - tiz wisht I tull ee" [I wouldn't go to that house at night - there is something strange about it I tell you]. The word "wisht" is probably derived from "bewitched".

wision vision

witch watch

wive wife

wommle wobble, disturbed, unsettled. A person with an upset stomach would say: "I'v got a wommle een me innerds."

wood'n wouldn't

woolvare welfare

wourd hoard, meaning saving - "They wourds ther money up." [They save their money.]

wud, wid would

wurdle world

wuss, wiss worse

wusser, wisser "worser" meaning - "worse than before".

wuz was

yark wild, stormy weather

yaw ewe [female sheep]

yemors embers, hot ashes

yer ear, hear, here, year, your. There is a story about the farm worker, who, on hearing strange noises coming from a rabbit hole, said to the farmer: "Yer maister, put yer yer yer an' yer wot yu can yer."

yerzel yourself

yet heat

yetty get warm or heated, to heat

yo "you" in Cornwall

yu you. Apart from the normal use of this word, it is also used frequently in the following fashion: "Oh ace yu." [Oh yes you.]

yullery yellow

yu'm you are

yushule usual

zackon second

zaffron caake saffron flavoured cake, popular in Devon and Cornwall. Two types of saffron cake are made; one is made with yeast, giving a texture like bread, the other is made in the usual manner. Small yeast buns flavoured with saffron are known as "nubbies".

zairious serious

zait seat

zam-zawed or zam-zawey a term applied to food or drink which has been prepared for some time and has become luke warm or tea which is stewed. (1750)

zar serve

zarmont sermon

zarternoon this afternoon

zartin certain

zarvin' serving

zarvint servant

zauft soft

zaw'd sewed

zaxon sexton

zayzide seaside

zeb'n seven

zed said

zeth saith, says

zee'd saw

zeed'n, zid'n saw him

zeed seed

zeedy caake seed cake, flavoured with carraway seeds

zengel single

zeptin' excepting, accepting

zex six

zex sect, such as "Methody" or "Church"

zide side, beside

zim-tims symtoms

zim seem, seam

zim'th seemeth, seems

zin seen .*See* **zeed.**

Zindy-go-t'Matein'
Sunday-go-to-Meeting.
Applied mostly to clothes kept for occasions of importance, but especially for going to Chapel. Also worn on social occasions, such as the Harvest Thanksgiving Tea. When these garments, including boots and "leggins" were replaced, they went down "one peg" and would be used for going to market or the annual "Zindy Skuel Trait" to the seaside. Mention must be made of the Harvest Thanksgiving Tea, which took place after the Thanksgiving Service. All parishoners took part - even some of those who were "Church" - contributing a variety of foodstuffs, but unlike today, a minimum of savouries.

A form of "one upmanship" was practised, each housewife endeavouring to supply "vittles" that would do her credit. The farmers' wives were at an advantage, because of being able to supply large bowls of clotted cream.

As in football, there were the "first division" farmers' wives and the "second division" housewives and labourers' wives. Whilst never voiced, it was understood by the community that the "first division" wives were better off and therefore, being the producers, were better able to supply the cream and butter. A general eye was kept on the "first division" baskets, the contents of which were expected to relate roughly to the acreage farmed. The "second division" supplied the less exotic fare and it was understood that it did the best it could afford.

When it was time for tea, the children went first, paying 3d each. Eyes darted swiftly over the table to make mental notes of the more desirable fare, [ie., sticky, jammy, creamy], so that one could pace oneself, keep an eye on the dwindling supply and select in the correct order. You were expected to start with bread and butter, jam and cream being allowed with this. There was none of the "genteel" putting of jam and cream on the side of the plate before transferring it to the bread and butter or splits, as is done in politer circles. Jam first, then cream was spread liberally and the largest mouthful taken because time was short. Having got through the bread stage, one worked as fast as possible through those items already marked - provided one was quick enough. The object was to try to "down" as much as possible in a given time, without appearing to be in the last stages of starvation. One was never quite sure how long one had - it depended on how many other children were waiting for "second sitting", or on some grown-up who would say, "Wull, av'ee aul ad 'nuff?" Of course, none of us had, but it was against tribal law to take another jam tart and cream, or other delicacy, no matter how much you wanted it. "Things would be said" about it and it was "just not done". We would all rise reluctantly from the trestle table, with what we were led to believe was the right inner feeling at the end of a meal - that one could eat a little more!

zing'th sings

zing'th out shouts or calls loudly

zing'd sang, sung

zitch such

zlatter'd scattered

zmurt smart

zode sold

zoonder a preference for, [the word "rather" would not be used].

zoo, zoe to let the cow go dry [stop its milk]. A Celtic word ; "*sych*" [Cornish and Welsh] ; "*suic*" [Irish] ; "*siccus*" [L].

zot sat

zowl a plough. Traceable to Saxon times, but was also "zool" or "zull" in advertisments in comparatively recent times. Originally, a "plough" meant a team or pair, of horses.

zpectin expecting, inspecting

zpowel spoil

ztidd'n studying or study it

ztrate street

zuddint sudden

zugs bogs, soft wet ground. *See* **stogged.**

zummat sooner

zune's as soon as

zwaip sweep

zwaller swallow

zwaatt sweat

zwaatt'n sweating